DOING *the* RIGHT THING

Also by Chuck Colson

Born Again
Loving God
Kingdoms in Conflict
Against the Night
Why America Doesn't Work (with Jack Eckerd)
The Body (with Ellen Vaughn)
Gideon's Torch (with Ellen Vaughn)
How Now Shall We Live? (with Nancy Pearcey)
Being the Body (with Ellen Vaughn)
God and Government
Charles Colson on Politics and the Christian Faith DVD
The Good Life (with Harold Fickett)
The Faith (with Harold Fickett)
The Faith DVD curriculum (with Garry Poole)

Also by Robert George

The Clash of Orthodoxies
In Defense of Natural Law
Embryo: A Defense of Human Life (with Christopher Tollefsen)
Making Men Moral: Civil Liberties and Public Morality

DOING *the* RIGHT THING

MAKING MORAL CHOICES IN A WORLD
FULL OF OPTIONS

PARTICIPANT'S GUIDE

SIX SESSIONS

CHUCK COLSON
AND ROBERT GEORGE

with GLENN SUNSHINE and T. M. MOORE

ZONDERVAN®

ZONDERVAN.com/
AUTHORTRACKER
follow your favorite authors

ZONDERVAN

Doing the Right Thing Participant's Guide
Copyright © 2011 by Charles W. Colson

Requests for information should be addressed to:
Zondervan, *Grand Rapids, Michigan 49530*

ISBN 978-0-310-42776-6

Cover design: Rob Monacelli
Interior design: Sherri Hoffman

Printed in the United States of America

11 12 13 14 15 16 /DCI/ 23 22 21 20 19 18 17 16 15 14 13 12 11 10 9 8 7 6 5 4 3 2 1

CONTENTS

Welcome   7

Session 1   How Did We Get into This Mess?   9

Session 2   Is There Truth, a Moral Law We All Can Know?   21

Session 3   If We Know What Is Right, Can We Do It?   35

Session 4   What Does It Mean to Be Human?   47

Session 5   Ethics in the Market Place   65

Session 6   Ethics in Public Life   79

Additional Resources   93

WELCOME

Welcome to *Doing the Right Thing,* a series of timely discussions on ethics in public life.

Over the next six sessions you will be drawn into conversations concerning some of the most important issues and challenges of our day. You will be led through this series by a distinguished panel of thinkers, writers, scholars, and ethicists, who will be assisted in their task by interviews with key thinkers and actors in a wide range of social and cultural arenas.

Over the six sessions of this series your thinking about ethics and morality will be profoundly challenged and, we hope, deeply enriched.

This participant's guide will be your companion and road map throughout this study. Prior to each session you should read through the introductory comments to prepare your mind for the discussions you will experience.

During the video panel discussion use the outline to make notes, jot down ideas and questions, or note passages of Scripture or incidents from your personal experience that come to mind. During the group discussion to follow you'll want to bring these questions and observations to the attention of your fellow participants.

Read through the group discussion questions section as part of your preparation each week. This will help keep you alert to items from the video panel discussions that can help in guiding your own group discussions.

Each session includes additional resources which you can consult for further insight into the issues discussed by the panel and in your group gathering. Also, follow-up questions and items for action to consider between sessions will lead you to begin taking more responsibility for the ethical climate of our times.

Doing the Right Thing will challenge you to become an active participant, not merely in a class on ethics, but in a movement that is seeking to revitalize moral life, renew culture, and restore ethical sanity to our society. Our prayer is that doing the right thing will become not just a good idea but, increasingly, a way of life for you and your fellow participants in this study.

How Did We Get into This Mess?

INTRODUCTION

A crisis of ethics

The United States is facing a serious crisis of ethics.

Perhaps the most obvious example of this is the recent financial crisis, where ethical lapses very nearly brought down the global financial system. Yet it is all too easy to blame the crisis on corporate greed and wrongdoing on Wall Street. Looking more closely at the situation, we find ethical problems on all levels, including on the part of the government and even individuals who took out mortgages they could not hope to repay, along with the banks and financial firms.

But what exactly is ethics? And how have our ethical standards so deteriorated that we don't even seem to know right from wrong? What are the consequences of these failures?

Standards of behavior: universal or relative?

Maybe the simplest operating definition is that ethics are standards of behavior, presumably derived from some objective source or transcendent authority, whether it is natural law or God. These standards regulate the conduct of our behavior and our relationships with one another. When sound standards are in place, transparency and honesty generally operate in financial and commercial markets. Obviously there are exceptions, but these become the norm for behavior.

Yet many in our society today reject the very notion of ethics as something that is either objective or universal. Instead, many have embraced the idea of moral and ethical relativism. This view holds that ethics are not based on transcendent truths, but are instead dependent on the situation and the people involved. Since there is no objective standard of right and wrong, all cultures are equal, all individual values are valid, and we cannot judge the choices that other people make. Even government cannot get involved in these questions because "there is no such thing as objective moral truth."

The impossibility of relativism

Relativism is a common view of ethics in many influential circles today, including business schools and academia in general, medical research labs, law schools, and halls of government. In our pluralistic world, it seems to many to be the only option.

The problem is, it doesn't work.

First, it is obvious that ethical failures occur. The outrage against executives at the financial services firms is ample evidence that we recognize wrongdoing. Yet if there is no objective ethical standard by which we can measure people's behavior, how can we even talk about unethical actions? There is no basis for judging anyone's actions as wrong or inappropriate. At best we can say they are illegal.

This leads directly to the second problem. In a world that believes in relativism, when obvious ethical lapses occur the only recourse is laws and government regulation. Yet regulations have loopholes and boundaries, whether by accident or design. No matter how carefully crafted regulations are, unethical people will find a way around the letter of the law and thus will not be restrained by them. Furthermore, increasing laws and regulations inevitably leads to an erosion of our freedoms.

So determining what ought to be and building a consensus around setting some ethical standards becomes essential for the survival of a free society. And developing this consensus and teaching it is critical for preventing the kinds of disastrous ethical failures that have caused so much havoc not only in the U.S., but internationally as well.

I. Ethical failures and the economic collapse

II. "The dictatorship of relativism"
   A. Business schools

   B. Creating a culture without ethics

III. Criminality

IV. "Borrowed capital" and ethical erosion

V. Resolving ethical disputes

SELLING SHORT is a way of making money when a stock declines in value. The short seller borrows a certain amount of stock from a broker and sells it; if the stock declines in value, the short seller buys it at the lower value, returns it to the broker, and keeps the difference in price less the borrowing fees. For example, the short seller could borrow 100 shares of a stock valued at $10 per share and sell them for $1,000; if the stock then drops to $8 per share, he could buy another 100 shares for $800, return them to the broker, and keep the $200 difference between the price he received for selling the shares and the price he paid to buy their replacements. If the stock goes up, the short seller will lose money. This is generally considered an ethical form of trade, though in the examples discussed here, the financial firms knew the assets were bad, sold them deceptively to companies that thought they were buying legitimate assets, and then shorted them to make a profit when they inevitably dropped in value. That action was clearly unethical on several levels.

14

QUESTIONS:

For Group Discussion

1. **Consider:** Brit Hume suggested that the financial collapse was caused by a widespread lack of, "first, ethical behavior by the government; second, ethical behavior in financial markets; third, ethical behavior by mortgage lending banks; and fourth, ethical behavior on the part of the public." Pope Benedict said, "The events of the last two or three years have demonstrated that the ethical dimension must enter into economic activity. Now is the time to see that ethics is not something external, but internal to economic rationality and pragmatism."

   Discuss: Read Exodus 20:15; Deuteronomy 25:13–16; and Luke 19:1–9. How do passages like these lead us to see that Christians should take more interest in ethics and the role of ethics in the economy?

2. **Consider:** Jim Grant argues that it is important to understand where the ethical failures on the part of government, business institutions, and even individuals occurred to allow for accountability and personal responsibility. Christians can sometimes be a little wary about "finger-pointing" because they don't want to "judge" others or their ethical values and practices.

   Discuss: How would you explain what Jesus meant in John 7:24, where He was quoting from Leviticus 19:15? Is it possible that as Christians, through our reluctance to be involved in matters of ethical judgment, we may also bear some responsibility for the crisis of ethics? Explain.

3. **Consider:** Chuck Colson claims it is impossible to teach ethics in business schools today. Donovan Campbell agrees that you need to subscribe to the idea of ultimate good or ultimate morality to provide a solid reference point for ethical decisions.

    Discuss: Read John 17:17 and Romans 7:12. Without an absolute standard of good, what kind of ethics can we teach?

4. **Consider:** Michael Miller claims that we are brought up to be relativists, then at some point are suddenly expected to act ethically when we have not been given a foundation for it.

    Discuss: Read Romans 2:14–15 and Titus 1:15. Is our conscience or our integrity a reliable starting point for ethics? Why or why not? What were you taught about right and wrong in school? Did you see more of an emphasis on *absolute* standards of right and wrong, or moral *relativism*?

5. **Consider:** The question that always arises when absolute morality is discussed is, whose morality? This problem is especially difficult when people who believe in absolute morality do not always hold to the same standards.

   Discuss: Based on what we've discussed thus far, where should Christians turn in order to begin thinking about ethics and morality? How can we resolve whatever differences may arise between us in considering these kinds of issues?

6. **Consider:** It is common in our culture to blame crime on poverty, racism, or some other form of institutionalized injustice.

   Discuss: If so, why is it that not everyone who experiences these things becomes a criminal? Read Matthew 15:19–20 and Romans 3:23. How do these passages account for criminal behavior?

QUESTIONS:

For Individual Reflection and Action between Sessions

1. Reflect on your own upbringing. When you were growing up, what lessons about morality did you learn from parents, teachers, and peers? Did any of those lessons point to absolutes? Did any encourage you in the way of relativism? List them below:

    Absolutes   **Relativism**

    Have you had more messages in one or the other of these areas? How has this shaped the decisions you've made in different areas of your life (social, financial, political, etc.)?

2. What is your personal reaction to the idea that there is an absolute standard of right and wrong that, as Donovan Campbell says, is true "outside of any context and which is translatable across cultures, times; it's applicable everywhere"?

If such a standard exists, what do you think it would look like? Where would you look to determine what it is?

What areas of your life would you need to reexamine in light of absolute ethical standards?

3. Review all the Scripture references provided for discussion in the first session. Would you say that Scripture encourages an absolute or relative ethic? How should this influence the way we think about our own ethical behavior?

4. The primary message of the first session is that America and the West are currently experiencing a crisis of ethics. In your own words, what is the nature of that crisis? Before the next class session, talk about this idea with some friends who are not in this course. Try to find out if they believe there is a crisis of ethics. How do they react to your suggesting this idea?

5. At ColsonCenter.org, read one or two of the additional resources listed below. The URLs are provided for your convenience in finding these articles.

ADDITIONAL RESOURCES

"Society Says, 'Relativism'," by Greg Koukl:
   http://www.colsoncenter.org/search-library/search?view=searchdetail&id=7346

"The Relativistic Fog: Why Moral Relativism Can't Be True," by Chuck Edwards:
   http://www.colsoncenter.org/search-library/search?view=searchdetail&id=4752

"How Hollywood Exploits Kids: The Dangers of Moral Relativism," by Charles Colson:
   http://www.colsoncenter.org/search-library/search?view=searchdetail&id=5257

Is There Truth, a Moral Law We All Can Know?

INTRODUCTION

Morality, ethics, and human rights

In our first session, Chuck Colson made the case that the idea of moral relativism makes it impossible to teach ethics, that there must be a commitment to transcendent moral truth for ethics to be possible. The concept that there is a moral law is the essential foundation for ideas of human rights, civil equality, and justice. This was Dr. Martin Luther King Jr.'s argument in his *Letter from the Birmingham Jail*, where he appealed to writers from the Christian natural law tradition to make the case that an unjust law does not bind the conscience, and that we have a moral responsibility to resist unjust laws.

The idea that there is a transcendent moral law is controversial today because of the influence of moral relativism, which teaches that there are no absolute standards of right and wrong, but that ideas of ethics come from culture and that right and wrong are determined by the situation rather than by any objective standards.

Natural law

In contrast, natural law ethics teaches that there is a moral law that is binding on all people, and that this law is knowable to human reason. So, for example, all societies have laws for marriage or something resembling it; the details may vary from culture to culture, but there is no society without norms for sexual relationships and child rearing. All societies have laws against theft and against murder. Most societies recognize some version of the Golden Rule. All of these are reflections of people's capacity to grasp certain human goods and reason about their implications for behaviors and the organization of society.

Christianity has historically argued that the natural law was given by God in whose image man is made. Because of human frailty and sin, we do not see the law as clearly as we should, and so divine revelation in Scripture helps to clarify it. Nonetheless, a significant segment of the Christian tradition, particularly within Catholic thought following St. Thomas Aquinas, holds that human reason is sufficient to develop an understanding of the fundamentals of ethics even apart from the Bible.

Natural law theory—Christian and otherwise—further argues that *positive law* (that is, human legislation) must be rooted in natural law for its legitimacy. Positive law is itself required by natural law for the protection of human goods and the well-being of all members of the community.

The need for consistency

The moral law must inform everything we do. We cannot compartmentalize it and only apply it in some areas of life while ignoring it in others. For example, when laws are unjust, when they do not conform to the moral law, we have a moral obligation to work to change them and to resist them if necessary through civil disobedience. This principle was at the heart of the Civil Rights movement as illustrated in Dr. King's *Letter from the Birmingham Jail*.

Failure to recognize and live by moral truth invites chaos in society. It can result in the worst injustices, including slavery, apartheid, and genocide, along with the kinds of behaviors that led to the economic crisis in the U.S. If we do not govern ourselves according to the moral law, government will have no choice but to legislate morality for us in the form of ever tighter laws and regulations of all aspects of our behavior. And that is the high road to tyranny.

I. Rev. Dr. Martin Luther King Jr.'s *Letter from the Birmingham Jail*
   A. The Judeo-Christian tradition

   B. Natural law

   C. Unjust laws and civil disobedience

II. The argument from experience
   A. C. S. Lewis, *The Abolition of Man*

   B. Children and fairness

III. Evolutionary psychology: is morality programmed into our genes?

    A. The argument from transformed behavior

    B. The argument from altruism

IV. Is moral relativism possible?

    A. Compartmentalization

    B. The problem of atrocities

    C. Religion in public life

    D. The problem of raw power in law and government

QUESTIONS:

For Group Discussion

1. **Consider:** In discussing Dr. King's *Letter from the Birmingham Jail*, Glenn Sunshine and Robert George both point to the Christian tradition as a major source for Dr. King's ideas about equality. Professor George argues that in principle, this idea is knowable to reason apart from Scripture.

   Discuss: Read Romans 2:14–15. What is, as the King James Version puts it, the "work of the law" and what does it mean to say this is "written" on the hearts of human beings? What would you cite as evidence that this is true?

2. **Consider:** Both the Bible and the natural law tradition argue for the "principle of equality, the equal worth of every human being, no matter how high or how low in the world's eyes, no matter how rich or poor, weak or strong, all being equal," as Professor George put it.

   Discuss: Read Genesis 1:26–28. What is the "image and likeness" of God? How does this factor into the belief in human equality before God? At the same time, in view of the immense differences between people in terms of ability or opportunity, how can we make the claim for human equality?

Discuss: Read Daniel 3:16–18; Acts 4:16–20; and Acts 5:27–29. How do you reconcile Dr. King's profound respect for law with his call to civil disobedience?

3. **Consider:** Christianity argues that natural law ethics comes from God and is written on the human heart, which is why there are so many similarities in ethical norms across cultures. Non-theists need a different explanation. One popular alternative today is evolutionary psychology, which argues that "natural law" is a result of natural selection, that is, that people who behaved this way had a survival advantage. Glenn Sunshine argued, however, that evolution occurs by the individual, not the group. In other words, according to Darwin, the individuals in a group that are better adapted for survival outcompete the others within their group and thus have the opportunity to pass their genes on to their heirs. But sacrificing yourself for the good of the group is not a trait that you can pass on to your heirs, and so it cannot be explained by Darwin's idea of survival of the fittest.

    Discuss: How does the existence of altruism (unselfish regard for the welfare of others) challenge the credibility of Darwinian evolution and the notion of "the survival of the fittest"? Is natural law theory a more satisfying explanation for altruism?

4. **Consider:** Michael Miller noted that people experience their ability to make choices every day. But if our behavior is programmed by our genes, free choice is not possible; all our choices are determined by genetic functions beyond our rational or moral control.

   Discuss: Where would you turn in the Bible to support the idea that human beings are individually morally accountable for their choices and works? Under the umbrella of Scripture, can anyone try to excuse his or her conduct by blaming genes? Explain.

5. **Consider:** In *The Abolition of Man*, C. S. Lewis makes the argument that natural law, which he calls the Tao, is the foundation for all other laws:

   This thing which I have called for convenience the Tao, and which others may call Natural Law or Traditional Morality or the First Principles of Practical Reason or the First Platitudes, is not one among a series of possible systems of value. It is the sole source of all value judgements. If it is rejected, all value is rejected. If any value is retained, it is retained. The effort to refute it and raise a new system of value in its place is self-contradictory. There has never been, and never will be, a radically new judgement of value in the history of the world. What purport to be new systems or (as they now call them) "ideologies", all consist of fragments from the Tao itself, arbitrarily wrenched from their context in the whole and then swollen to madness in their isolation, yet still owing to the Tao and to it alone such validity as they possess.

Discuss: In view of Romans 2:14–15 and the cultural and moral relativism common in our culture, what do you think of Lewis's argument? Are all systems of value, all concepts of right and wrong ultimately derived from the same source? What are the sources from which we can learn moral truth?

6. **Consider:** Michael Miller argues that we have only two choices: either questions about the nature of humanity and the common good are settled on the basis of truth, or they are settled on the basis of power. The only hope for those holding minority views on ethical matters is that the political powers-that-be will act favorably toward them.

   Discuss: Read Leviticus 5:1; Proverbs 15:22–23 and 25:26. In a pluralistic society, is it appropriate to advocate for your ethical beliefs even if informed by a religion or worldview that others may not accept? Why or why not?

QUESTIONS:

For Individual Reflection and Action between Sessions

1. From what sources do you draw your ethics? If you think of yourself as a relativist, ask yourself if you have ever made a judgment about another person's behavior. If you have, have you implicitly appealed to an ethical standard that transcends your personal moral code? How can you know whether such judgments are sound?

2. What are some of the standards that guide your understanding of ethics? You might find it helpful to think about this in terms of the different spheres of your life: your spouse, your children, your parents, your work, your finances, your leisure, your personal life, etc.

   If everyone followed your ethics, what would the consequences be? Compile a list of what you might consider your "rock-bottom ethical nonnegotiables." Then, go back to your list and prioritize them, highest to lowest. Finally, see if you can justify these values from Scripture.

3. The primary message of this lesson is that it is difficult, if not impossible, to be a consistent moral relativist. Everyone seems to appeal to universal or absolute moral standards, if only implictly. As you read or watch the news this week, listen for indications of either relativist or absolutist norms in the reports. Jot down examples of each below:

Relativist   **Absolutist**

4. At ColsonCenter.org, read one or two of the additional resources listed on page 33. The URLs are provided for your convenience in finding these articles.

ADDITIONAL RESOURCES

"It's a Natural," by Charles Colson:
http://www.colsoncenter.org/search-librarysearch?view=searchdetail&id=242

"In Whose Image," by Stephen H. Webb:
http://www.colsoncenter.org/search-library/search?view=searchdetail&id=5689

"Night of the Living Dead: Why We're Not Zombies," by Charles Colson:
http://www.colsoncenter.org/search-library/search?view=searchdetail&id=296

IF WE KNOW WHAT IS RIGHT, CAN WE DO IT?

INTRODUCTION

But can we do it?

In the last session, we saw that, though people of faith will generally look to their religious traditions for ethical guidance, there is an objective moral law that we can know through reason. This is known as natural law ethics, and it provides a common foundation for ethics even in pluralistic societies.

But once we have our idea of right and wrong, the question arises of whether or not we can do the right thing. Why is it that even when we know what is right, we sometimes choose to do otherwise? And how do we change our actions so that they better align with the good?

Training in virtue

C. S. Lewis's book *The Abolition of Man* once again helps us to understand the problem. Lewis explains that our appetites and desires (our "belly") need to be under the control of reason (our "head") if we are to live a well-ordered life. But given the strength of our appetites, reason by itself is insufficient to control them. The head thus needs "the chest" to govern the belly. Our "chest" is "the seat of emotions trained by habit" to pursue virtue. The problem in our society, which Lewis saw coming in 1943 when he published the book, is that we have rejected the idea of training people in virtue and then are shocked when people do wrong.

This is played out in the "ethical lapses" we see in government and business, where moral relativism has replaced moral truth in people's education. It is also seen in our rising incarceration rates as shown by Richard Herrnstein and James Q. Wilson, who concluded that crime is caused by lack of moral training in the morally formative years.

Habits of the heart

The solution, then, would seem to be to develop habits of the heart that lead to right behavior. This, in turn, requires two things. The first is what Dr. Samenow refers to as "conversion." This isn't necessarily religious, but does involve a radical change in the direction of life away from vice and toward virtue. In order for that to happen, however, both history and experience tell us that some form of community support is necessary.

When societies have a moral consensus, all the different communal groups work to support and reinforce core moral messages. The first and most important communal group is the family, which provides the essential moral foundation for the child. These moral concepts are reinforced in school through a curriculum that taught and modeled virtue. Other civic groups such as the Boy Scouts and Girl Scouts, the YMCA, the Knights of Columbus, or the Rotary Club—the organizations philosopher Edmund Burke called the "little platoons"—all simultaneously reinforce ethical norms and build cohesion in the society.

Institutional disarray

None of these institutions are functioning as well as they should in American life today. We face an unprecedented breakdown in the family, education often seems more concerned to undermine the foundations of moral belief than to promote ethical conduct, civic groups are facing a major decline and in many places have been replaced by gangs, and so on. No wonder, then, that we are facing an ethical crisis today.

We can learn to live ethically, but it requires several things of us. First, we must begin a process of education so that our hearts as well as our minds can be schooled in virtue. Second, we must make a firm commitment to live ethically and to make right behavior a habit in our hearts. And to take these steps, we must find others who will work with us, tell us the truth about ourselves and our choices, and support us in our efforts to live more ethically.

Video Notes Outline

I. The danger of self-righteousness

II. The properly ordered soul
   A. Reason and the passions

   B. Conversion

   C. "The chest"

III. Developing integrity
   A. The paradox

   B. The role of community

C. The nature of freedom

D. The conscience

E. The virtues

IV. Community and accountability
    A. Marines

    B. Inner-change freedom initiative in prisons

    C. Family

    D. Alexis de Tocqueville and community groups

QUESTIONS:

For Group Discussion

1. **Consider:** C. S. Lewis argued that reason must govern passion, for we cannot trust our passions — or our heart — as a reliable source of ethical decision-making.

   Discuss: Read Jeremiah 17:9; Proverbs 4:23; and Matthew 15:16–20. On the basis of these passages, should we agree with Lewis? Why or why not? How should your answer affect the way you make ethical choices and decisions?

2. **Consider:** Lewis said that the mind can only govern the heart through the chest. By this he meant that once moral convictions have been learned and internalized, these convictions can use good judgment and sound reason to control the passions.

   Discuss: The Scriptures use the idea of "conscience" where Lewis wrote of the "chest." Read the following passages: Hebrews 9:14; 1 Timothy 4:1–2; Romans 2:15; 1 Corinthians 8:7, 12; Hebrews 10:22; and 1 Timothy 1:5. What is the conscience and how is it supposed to work in relation to the mind and the heart? How would you suggest that a person might strengthen his or her conscience?

3. **Consider:** The panelists argued that true freedom involves the use of reason; it is not simply freedom from external control of our behavior. We must therefore use our minds to control our emotions, even though most people seem to let their emotions control their minds.

   Discuss: Read Romans 12:1–2 and 1 Peter 1:13. What does it mean to "be renewed" in our minds and to "prepare" our minds for right ethical action? Discuss some parameters of a regimen of exercises or disciplines that one might adopt in order to realize this objective.

4. **Consider:** Robert George said that growing in ethics is a paradox: no one can do it for you, but at the same time you cannot do it on your own. Communities and groups can be important for helping us act in an ethical way, but group members must be intentional toward one another to this end. Today, many of the "mediating structures"—groups—in our society that should be helping us live ethically are in disarray.

   Discuss: Read the following passages: John 13:34–35; 1 Corinthians 12:24–25; Galatians 6:2; Ephesians 5:18–21; Colossians 3:16; 1 Thessalonians 5:11; and Hebrews 10:24. What recurrent phrase do you identify in these verses? Taking all these verses together, what do they teach about the kinds of "groups" or "communities" that might strengthen us to live in a more ethical manner?

5. **Consider:** Accountability to others can be an important resource for integrity and ethical accountability. Chuck Colson suggests having a circle of close friends to help you make important decisions and to hold you accountable in various ways.

   Discuss: Considering the various passages of Scripture we've examined in this lesson, how might a group of close friends help one another to grow in mind, heart, conscience, and ethical living? What would such an accountability relationship look like? How might you take steps to put such a group in place in your life?

6. **Consider:** Dr. Samenow argued that the solution to criminal behavior is conversion, that is, reorienting a convict's life and ethos away from criminal behavior and toward an ethically sound way of life. Talk about some people you know, either contemporary or historical figures, who have undergone this kind of conversion.

   Discuss: What does "conversion" mean in Christian terms. Read Ephesians 4:17–24. Is Christian conversion a "one-time" or an ongoing experience? Explain your answer. Do you think that real and lasting conversion can occur in a wholly secular or unbelieving situation?

QUESTIONS:

For Individual Reflection and Action between Sessions

1. Between now and the next session, pay special attention to the way your reason and emotions interact on various matters during the course of a day. Make some notes about ways you felt, what you were thinking, and how your conscience acted in various situations. Reflect on what you perceive to be the overall state of your soul — the interaction of mind, heart, and conscience according to the priorities, values, and teaching of Scripture.

2. What obstacles can keep you from becoming more consistent in how you think about ethical questions? That is, what can get in the way of your growing in how you think, feel, will, and act with respect to the teaching of the moral law of God? How might you begin to overcome these obstacles?

3. Most people do not have a close-knit support group they can turn to for accountability and moral formation. Do you have such a group? If not, whom could you ask to be an accountability partner with you? Do you have a group of people in your life who share your interests in living a life of greater integrity and with whom you could form a support group? List any names that

come to mind and commit to contact them to discuss this possibility during the coming week.

4. The primary message of this lesson is that sound ethics requires good judgment via a good conscience in the context of healthy support groups and communities. Review all the Scripture discussed in this lesson. On the basis of these passages, what can you do to begin helping your fellow Christians become more consistent in their ethical thinking and behavior? In other words, as part of a community of people called to a particular ethic, what is your responsibility as a contributing member of such a community?

5. At ColsonCenter.org, read one or two of the additional resources listed on page 46. The URLs are provided for your convenience in finding these articles.

"The Nurture of the Soul," by T. M. Moore:
http://www.colsoncenter.org/search-library/search?view=searchdetail&id=1917

"A Soul Is a Terrible Thing to Waste: More Than Education," by Charles Colson:
http://www.colsoncenter.org/search-library/search?view=searchdetail&id=11725

"Learning Character: How Not to Raise a Barbarian," by Charles Colson:
http://www.colsoncenter.org/search-library/search?view=searchdetail&id=12030

WHAT DOES IT MEAN TO BE HUMAN?

INTRODUCTION

Critical questions

One of the most contentious and difficult areas of ethics today revolves around the related fields of medical ethics and biotechnology. These fields raise many questions. On the medical front, how should we allocate medical resources? Should decisions be based on a patient's ability to pay or should we guarantee some standard of care to everyone? If we choose the latter, who determines what that minimum standard of care is? How should we handle shortages of medical supplies or personnel? Who makes end-of-life decisions? Who pays for treatment? These are critical questions that cross the boundaries between ethics, economics, psychology, sociology, business, and politics.

In the biotech field, the questions are just as big. Is it ever right to take a life in order to create or to save one? Because science can do something, should it? Is it appropriate to use genetic testing to determine whether or not a baby should be carried to term? If so, are there any limits to this testing? Can we select for gender, hair and eye color, etc., or should we be limited to serious health issues? Is disability an adequate reason for abortion? If so, which disabilities? Does color blindness count?

The central question

Hovering over all of these questions is the central question, what does it mean to be human? Are human beings fundamentally different from animals? Is there a difference between a human being and a person, and if so, who gets to decide what it is? Do human beings all have equal dignity and value, or are some more valuable and deserving of more rights (and medical care) than others?

Historically, the Western ideal has been that all people are equal and have equal worth and dignity. This idea, which has its origins in the biblical teaching that human beings are made in the image of God, is clearly articulated in the Declaration of Independence: "We hold these truths to be self-evident, that all men are created equal, that they are endowed by their Creator with certain unalienable rights, that among these are Life, Liberty, and the Pursuit of Happiness...."

Increasingly, the idea that all human beings have equal rights has been questioned, typically by denying that human beings at some stage of development (the embryonic, the fetal) or in some conditions are "persons." This distinction allows the rights of some human beings to be preserved while allowing for the destruction of others, whether for convenience, concern about handicaps or "quality of life," or to "harvest" spare parts. The justification for this is usually based on a utilitarian calculus of looking for the greatest good for the greatest number. While this idea may sound reasonable on the surface, it can and has led to horrendous abuses in the name of scientific advancement of society because it undermines the foundation of human rights.

As we face questions of bioethics, we need to do so with a firm insistence on the inherent and equal value and worth of each individual, drawing from the natural law tradition as well as Scripture.

VIDEO NOTES OUTLINE

I. Dr. Swan and battlefield triage

II. Allocating resources

    A. Image of God and human dignity

    B. Eugenics

    C. The principle of double effect

III. Making medical decisions

    A. The problem of cost

B. The problem of socialized medicine

C. Family decisions vs. state decisions

IV. Questions of bioethics
   A. Designer babies for spare parts

   B. Embryo-destructive stem cell research

   C. Human vs. person

V. What does it mean to be human?

   A. Unique dignity of each person as the foundation for dealing with medical and bioethical issues

   B. Peter Singer's utilitarianism

DOUBLE EFFECT: The principle of double effect takes account of the fact that often our actions have multiple consequences, some good, some bad. Where an act can be foreseen to have consequences of both types, the principle of double effect distinguishes between those that are *intended*, and those that are unintended *side effects*. A consequence can be intended two ways, as an *end* or as a *means* to an end. So, for example, one intends someone's death as an end when one deliberately kills someone out of hatred; one intends someone's death as a means to an end when one kills someone to inherit money from the victim's will.

The principle is applied, for example, to distinguish suicide from acts of heroism. Imagine that a person hates his life and decides to end it by blowing himself up. That is intending something bad—one's own death. But we think differently about the case of a brave soldier who, to save the lives of his comrades, dives on a grenade that has been lobbed into his camp by an enemy. He knows that his act will have among its effects his own death. But that is not what he is intending—either

53

as end or means. What he is intending is the saving of the lives of his fellow soldiers. His act has two effects, one good, one bad. The good one is intended; the bad one is a side effect.

The principle is also applied in considering acts that cause the death of an unborn baby. "Direct" abortion—that is, abortion in which the purpose of the act is to destroy the developing child—is always wrong because it involves intending the baby's death. But sometimes an unborn baby's death is the unintended, albeit foreseen and accepted, consequence of an act whose purpose is saving the life of the mother. Consider, for example, the case of a pregnant woman who is diagnosed with a virulent uterine cancer at a point at which her baby cannot survive outside the womb. To save her life, let us suppose, it is necessary to remove her uterus immediately. The act will have two effects: the survival of the mother and the death of her child. Christian teaching—whether Catholic, Orthodox, or Protestant—has long held that in such a case the bad effect is outside the scope of intention and the act of removing the cancerous uterus is not properly classified as an abortion (or a direct abortion).

How can we distinguish "intending as a means" from "accepting as a side effect"? Often we can tell by asking whether the act would be successful, and regarded as such by the actor, if somehow the anticipated bad effect was not produced. So, for example, in the case of the brave soldier, what if his body muffled the grenade so perfectly that he actually survived the incident? Would he have accomplished his goal? Or was his death part of the goal? The answer is clear: he would have accomplished his goal—saving his buddies—and would have considered his own survival to have in no way frustrated his objective.

In the case of the cancerous uterus, we could ask: Would one remove the cancerous organ if the woman were not pregnant (meaning an unborn baby would not die as a result of the removal)? Presumably, the answer is yes. But that shows that one's intention is not destroying the baby, but rather saving the life of the mother. If, somehow, the baby were to survive, one would have accomplished all that one set out to do—i.e., save the woman from the cancer. The failure to produce a dead child would not render the act unsuccessful. Contrast this with the case of a genuine ("direct") abortion—if the act is performed and somehow the baby survives, the abortionist failed in his mission. He did not accomplish the goal he set out to achieve—namely, killing the child.

It is important to understand that the norm against intending a bad consequence is not the only moral norm. An act may be wrongful for other reasons. So, in the case of killing, for example, an act in which death is a foreseen but unintended consequence may nevertheless be morally impermissible because it violates some other principle of morality. For example, even in accepting unintended but foreseen bad consequences it is morally required that one respect the norms of justice and fairness. Sometimes the Golden Rule forbids one from imposing on others a bad consequence, even as a side effect.

UTILITARIANISM: According to Jeremy Bentham, the founding father of utilitarianism, moral acts are those which produce the greatest good for the greatest number. Bentham's utilitarianism was hedonistic—he identified "good" with pleasure and "bad" with pain. Contemporary utilitarians have generally abandoned the identification of the good with pleasure, or with pleasure alone. They have, however, retained the idea that the *consequences* of acts are all that matter in moral evaluation, and that consequences can be compared with each other and quantified to enable us to resolve moral questions by a process of determining which choice or act will yield the net best proportion of good to bad (however good and bad are defined—obviously, this method cannot itself settle what is to count as good and bad). The great Christian philosopher Elizabeth Anscombe labeled this method "consequentialist."

The master moral principle of contemporary consequentialists is that people should choose that action which promises overall and in the long run to produce the net best proportion of benefit to harm. There are no other absolutes. As a result, utilitarians and other consequentialists typically reject the proposition (affirmed by classical philosophers as well as Jewish and Christian thinkers) that some acts (such as rape or the direct killing of innocent human beings) are intrinsically morally evil and can never be justified by their consequences.

Critics of consequentialists, including Christian critics, argue that consequentialist methodology is unworkable. Many of the things we see as good (or bad) can be neither quantified nor meaningfully compared with each other in ways that enable the consequentialist method to work. Further, consequences matter in moral evaluation, but so do intentions and other factors. The critics also argue that there are moral norms that do not have any exceptions (or what are sometimes called "moral absolutes"), contrary to consequentialist claims.

QUESTIONS:

For Group Discussion

1. **Consider:** Utilitarianism is based on the idea that there are no moral absolutes, but that ethical behavior is based on working to produce the greatest good (or the greatest happiness) for the greatest number.

   Discuss: Scripture claims to be able to equip us for every good work (2 Timothy 3:15–17) and to enable us to know the truth (John 17:17). Given such claims, do you think utilitarianism is a good foundation for ethics? Why or why not? What would you propose as a basis for making ethical decisions?

2. **Consider:** Professor Peter Singer, who teaches at Princeton, said, "When the death of a disabled infant will lead to the birth of another infant with better prospects of a happy life, the total amount of happiness will be greater if the disabled infant is killed. The loss of a happy life for the first infant is outweighed by the gain of a happier life for the second. Therefore, if killing the hemophiliac infant has no adverse effect on others, it would, according to the total view, be right to kill him."

   Discuss: Read Matthew 19:13–14 and Acts 2:37–39. How would Jesus and the apostles respond to Dr. Singer? Do children with handicaps have a right to live? Do they have a right to be born? Why or why not?

3. **Consider:** The goal of utilitarian ethics is to increase "the total amount of happiness." Yet we must wonder how such an idea might be measured. For example, someone would have to determine, by some agreed-upon means, how to balance the resources (people, time, money) spent in working to find a treatment for spinal cord injuries against the use of those same resources to provide clean drinking water to thousands of people in Haiti. In a utilitarian system, it might be difficult to construct a framework to protect the rights of individuals. Which of those rights, for example, would be "inalienable?" And for whom?

   Discuss: Review the discussion from session 2 on the image of God. Reflect also on Psalm 139:13–17. In what ways does having this concept "on the table" help to overcome some of the problems of a utilitarian approach to matters of "life"?

4. **Consider:** Certain ethical views want to make a distinction between being a human being and being a person, supposing that such a distinction might help in resolving some difficult ethical issues. Dr. Rae distinguished between *being* a person and *functioning* as a person. We can probably all think of examples where this kind of logic might be introduced in matters relating to life and the "quality of life."

   Discuss: Read 2 Samuel 9:1–13 and Romans 12:8–10. How many "strikes" did Mephibosheth possibly have against him in David's eyes? How do you account for David's treatment of him?

Discuss: If not all human beings are persons, who gets to decide who is and who isn't? How would you argue the point that *you* are both a human being and a person?

5. **Consider:** Father Sirico discussed the idea of double effect, which claims that it is ethically valid under some circumstances to pursue a good end knowing that some evil may result as a side effect. Later, Michael Miller states that we cannot "do evil to attain some good." We need to recognize that there is a clear difference between double effect and doing evil to attain a good.

   Discuss: Read Romans 3:7–8 and Romans 6:1–2. How would Paul respond to the idea of doing evil to attain some good? Under what circumstances is it appropriate to do medical research on human subjects? When does it cross the line from double effect to doing evil so that good may result? Here are some specific situations for you to discuss:

   • Is there an ethical difference between taking a kidney from someone without their consent if the person is fully functional vs. if the person is in a coma? Is there a difference between the latter and destroying an embryo to obtain stem cells for a medical treatment or for research? What does your answer say about what you think gives a person human rights?

   • Is it ethically justifiable to produce a baby for spare parts for another sibling?

- In light of the distinction between double effect and doing evil to produce a good, where do you think euthanasia falls? Why? Who should make end-of-life decisions?

6. **Consider:** Widespread use of genetic testing has resulted in a massive reduction in the number of children with Down's Syndrome born in the U.S.; rather than being born, Down's babies are being aborted. This practice will effectively exterminate the next generation of Down's children.

   Divide into groups of three and discuss one of the following cases, using the scriptural teaching we have considered thus far in this series:

   - **Discuss (1):** What do you think are the ethical and practical issues involved in these decisions? What do you think that communicates to people with Down's and their families? Do you know anyone with Down's Syndrome? If so, how would you describe them?

   - **Discuss (2):** The eugenics movement was an effort to improve on future generations by not allowing the "unfit" to have children. Do you think this is a worthwhile goal? Is there any relationship between these ideas and our current focus on genetic testing and abortion for the severely handicapped?

- **Discuss (3):** The most common piece of high tech medical equipment in many developing countries is an ultrasound machine. It is used to determine the sex of a developing fetus, allowing the family to abort the baby if it is a girl. Is this an appropriate use of technology? Families in the U.S. can abort freely, for any reason, and especially if the baby will cause them hardship (e.g., Down's Syndrome); since girls pose a financial hardship in many developing countries, what is the difference between those situations and a handicapped child in the U.S.?

- **Discuss (4):** Another example of current eugenics-inspired practices is in the market for sperm and egg donations from people of specified ethnicity, height, hair and eye color, educational achievement, etc., for in vitro fertilization and implantation. What are the ethical implications of this practice?

- **Discuss (5):** Given that eugenics resulted in forced sterilizations and ultimately contributed to the Holocaust, should these trends worry us? What potential problems (e.g., with medical insurance) might come from our current forms of eugenics?

QUESTIONS:

For Individual Reflection and Action between Sessions

1. Discuss with your family which medical treatments you would want done and which you would refuse in the event of a medical crisis that leaves you unable to communicate. What factors enter into your decisions?

2. In light of this session, have any of your attitudes toward people or issues changed? What can you do to advocate for a more just society that reflects the unique dignity of every human life? What adjustments do you need to make in your own attitudes, words, or actions to better reflect the value of every human life? Whom can you bring on board to help you move in this direction?

3. Imagine that you have been asked to teach a group of elementary school children from your church how to respond to a "special needs" child who has just moved to the community and will be "mainstreamed" into their class. What should the "special needs" child expect from the other children? How should current class members prepare themselves to demonstrate the love of Christ to this new child?

4. The primary message of this lesson is that every human life has value and dignity. Review the Scripture passages cited in this lesson. Put them all together into a single statement of no more than three sentences to explain what the Bible teaches about the sanctity of life.

5. At ColsonCenter.org, read one or two of the additional resources listed below. The URLs are provided for your convenience in finding these articles.

ADDITIONAL RESOURCES

"Life in Three Dimensions," by James R. Edwards:
   http://www.colsoncenter.org/search-library/search?view=searchdetail&id=2617

"Terminal Logic," by Robert P. George:
   http://www.colsoncenter.org/search-library/search?view=searchdetail&id=14805

"Completely Pro-Life: Fearfully and Wonderfully Made," by Charles Colson:
   http://www.colsoncenter.org/search-library/search?view=searchdetail&id=5866

ETHICS IN THE MARKET PLACE

INTRODUCTION

The crisis in business

Nowhere is the ethical crisis in America more obvious than in business. Companies such as Enron and Tyco have become synonymous with corporate corruption, and entire industries from mortgage brokers to financial services to Wall Street have been pilloried as hopelessly self-serving and greedy.

And while some companies are failing or barely surviving, their executives receive lavish salaries, perks, and bonuses.

Is the current ethical crisis in business an inevitable result of an emphasis on greed peculiar to capitalism, or is it possible to build an ethical center for business that will keep the market economy functioning properly? Or, to put it differently, what is the purpose of business? Is it simply to make money, or is there something more that it is supposed to do in society?

Free market economics

To answer this question, we need to look at the basics of free market economics. In a free market system, businesses exist to provide goods and services to the public. The public, in turn, is free to decide where and on what they will spend their money. They choose which goods and services they want and from whom they will buy them. Businesses compete for customers; the money a business makes is a measure of the value it provides to the public.

In other words, business does not exist purely to make money, but to provide products and services to the public, for which it is rewarded with profit.

It is thus a mistake to say that capitalism is built on greed. It is true that the profit motive is built into the system, but profit isn't (or shouldn't be) the sole driving force in business. In fact, free market systems can encourage the development of a variety of virtues: the rule of law, trust, thrift, hard work, service, responsible risk, perseverance, etc.

Greed and selfishness

Unfortunately, however, greed and selfishness are universal human problems that plague all political, social, and economic systems. As a result, problems with greed and lust for power can easily distort the free market system: monopolies, which eliminate competition, can lead to artificially high prices; unsafe manufacturing practices can lead to inferior or dangerous products; workers can be exploited to maximize profit; government action can artificially prop up or penalize businesses; excessive regulation (often in response to abuses) can hurt competitiveness and drive up costs for consumers; inadequate regulation can result in exploitation of employees, consumers, or the environment.

How do we avoid these problems? Theologian Michael Novak argues that Western liberal democracies are built on a three-legged stool consisting of political freedom, economic freedom, and moral restraint. Remove any one leg and the stool will collapse. Without ethics, without moral restraint in the populace, in business, and in government, the system will collapse and we will lose our political and economic freedom.

This means that it is vitally important to recover ethics in business and the economy if we want to maintain a free society and to encourage the virtues that free markets can bring.

Video Notes Outline

I. "Obsessive individualism"

   A. The imperial self

   B. Greed and virtue

II. Essential business values

   A. Trust

   B. Vision

   C. Stewardship

D. Moral values

III. Business and the common good
    A. Doing the right thing: Bob Rowling/Omni Hotels

    B. Doing the right thing: Doug DeVos/Amway Corporation

    C. Potential for harm

    D. Corporate social responsibility vs. ethics

    E. Making a contribution

IV. No perfect system

CORPORATE SOCIAL RESPONSIBILITY (CSR) is a movement
that seeks to integrate a particular set of values into corporate
business models so that they police themselves in the selected
areas. This typically includes an emphasis on a "triple bottom
line" of the environment, people (employees, consumers, and
anyone affected by the corporation's actions), and profit. It encourages companies to integrate the public interest — defined
in terms of these categories, as well as community development — into all of their decisions.

QUESTIONS:

For Group Discussion

1. **Consider:** One of the overarching themes of this session is that business operating in a free market environment can be a force for good in society. There are obviously many examples to demonstrate that this is true.

    Discuss: Think about the businesses and businessmen and businesswomen you know. Do they demonstrate ways that people in the market place can act in an ethical manner? Would you say the majority do or do not? Do you think society benefits from these businesses? If so, how?

    Discuss: If a legitimate business makes a profit for its owner, does this help or hurt the local community economically? Can a person get rich only by impoverishing other people, or is it possible for a person to attain wealth while at the same time improving the economy more broadly? In other words, do businesses contribute to the common good or only to their owners' good? Explain your answer.

2. **Consider:** In previous generations, employees who did their jobs well typically had good job security, especially in major corporations. In return, employees were generally loyal to their company. That's not as true today as it used to be, and the desire for money—on the part of employers and employees—has been a major factor in undermining job loyalty and security. Ben Stein commented, "The real problem ... is the manager who really believes he has only one obligation. That obligation is to just make as much money as fast as he can, and get the heck out of there before anybody catches him. I mean, that's sort of how it's done. It's not based on trying to have any kind of long-term plan for helping the country or the company or the employees or the stockholders. It's just, 'How can I loot this company for myself?'"

   Discuss: How does the Christian ethic of loving your neighbor and doing unto others as you would have them do unto you address the problem of "obsessive individualism"? Read Proverbs 4:20–27. Suggest some ways that a text like this might provide a foundation for ethical practices in the market place. How would you apply some of the principles of this text to such things as leading others, serving the community, and making purchases?

3. **Consider:** Brit Hume commented, "It is perhaps the genius of the capitalist system that it harnesses the natural tendency toward greed in such a way that no greedy and successful businessman or entrepreneur can accomplish his or her goals without other people. So you have to build a large enterprise. If you want

to make more money you have to expand it. In order to do that, you need other people. You need people to come and build your buildings for you, you need people to come and work for you, you need people to come and buy your equity. If you do well, they do well. Jobs are created; it's how the whole thing works. So, in a very real sense, vice is harnessed to a virtuous outcome."

Discuss: Read Matthew 25:14–30. What is profit? Is profit legitimate? Necessary? Do you think desire for profit is necessarily the same as greed? Is it a vice? Is there a downside to pursuit of profit?

4. **Consider:** Scott Rae and Michael Miller both make the point that successful market economies depend on structural elements in society such as private property and the rule of law, but also on personal characteristics on the part of business owners.

   Discuss: Read Exodus 20:2–17. Discuss ways that these ethical guidelines might help breed positive ethical behavior into the market place in a community. Look also at Matthew 22:34–40. What does this add to the discussion of ethics in the market place?

5. **Consider:** Father Sirico talked about the social and moral dimensions of work and of business, pointing out that markets always involve interaction between people, and that few other things touch as many aspects of human life. Given this moral dimension of business, it would seem to be very important that we try to shore up the ethical foundations of business.

Some might insist that only government can do this, and that therefore we need more government intervention in the market place.

Another model says that the answer can be found within corporations themselves. David Miller suggests adjusting compensation for more than just the financial bottom line as a way to incentivize right behavior, as some corporations already do — another example of harnessing the profit motive to produce a positive social benefit.

On the other hand, Michael Miller argues that this can be taken in the wrong direction. He says that the Corporate Social Responsibility movement is a disaster for business ethics because "one, it substitutes actual questions of right and wrong and good and bad, with what's politically or socially fashionable at the time. Two, it's relativistic.... The money usually goes to different groups and it ultimately ends up being a protection racket. So that it's like a new transaction cost of doing business in the United States. You have to pay off the greens, and the Catholics, and the pro-aborts and the anti-aborts, and the hunters and PETA, so that they just leave you alone so that you can do business." He argues that simply changing the system won't fix the problem.

Professor George suggests that we stigmatize bad behavior, as has been done with tobacco companies.

Brit Hume said that maybe the answer was that "at the top of these organizations, you need virtuous people." Author and teacher Dr. John C. Maxwell has similarly argued, "There's no such thing as business ethics. There's just ethics. Either you have them or you don't. And if you have them, they'll work in business."

Discuss: Look at Ephesians 4:17–24 and Romans 12:1–2. What's the relationship between being a disciple of Jesus Christ and ethics in the market place? Does your church teach discipleship with a broad enough scope to equip church members to live and work ethically in the market place? Why or why not?

Questions:

For Individual Reflection and Action between Sessions

1. Talk to an entrepreneur or small business owner you know and ask her or him what it takes to succeed in their business. What personality traits are particularly important? Would you consider these vices or virtues?

2. Think about your own work situation. What ethical issues have come up? How have they been handled? What can you do to improve the ethical climate where you work?

3. How can consumers affect the practice of ethics in the market place? Which of your consuming practices seem to have some ethical component to them?

4. The primary message of this lesson has been that ethics in the market place must be concerned about more than merely making money. Review all the Scripture passages referenced in this lesson. See if you can draw up a list of "Ten Commandments" to guide your own ethical involvement in the market place.

5. At ColsonCenter.org, read one or two of the additional resources listed below. The URLs are provided for your convenience in finding these articles.

ADDITIONAL RESOURCES

"Biblical Foundations of Business Ethics," by Hershey H. Friedman:
http://www.colsoncenter.org/search-library/search?view=searchdetail
&id=6891

"Business and Ethics," by Ray Cotton:
http://www.colsoncenter.org/search-library/search?view=searchdetail
&id=13761

"Same Old, Same Old: The Demise of Business Ethics," by Charles Colson:
http://www.colsoncenter.org/search-library/search?view=searchdetail
&id=14772

ETHICS IN PUBLIC LIFE

INTRODUCTION

Absolutely untrustworthy

We are all familiar with problems of corruption and unethical behavior in government. British historian Lord Acton observed, "Power tends to corrupt, and absolute power corrupts absolutely." Acton was speaking out of a long tradition, going back into the Middle Ages, of reflection on the relationship between the Christian doctrine of original sin—the idea that people have a natural bent toward evil—and government. Because all people are prone to sin, some medieval thinkers argued that no one could be trusted with absolute power, and that there needed to be limited government with a system of checks and balances in place to hinder rulers from abusing their authority.

Aside from structural checks on the power of rulers, certain Christian philosopers and theologians also argued that all people had certain God-given rights that preceded the institution of human government, including particularly the rights to life, liberty, and property. Since these were given by God, government has no authority over them and cannot arbitrarily take them away from anyone.

These ideas, of course, influenced the writing of the Declaration of Independence, which argued that government exists specifically to defend our inalienable rights. The same ideas also shaped the U.S. Constitution, with its separation of powers, its system of checks and balances, and its concept of limited government. To further drive home the point that our rights have their origin outside of government, the Bill of Rights was soon adopted to define certain "negative rights," that is, rights that could not be abridged by the federal government.

Government and justice

The Founders were aware, however, that even the best governmental structure in the world could not prevent corruption if we failed to elect virtuous leaders to government. We have not always done so, leading Mark Twain to quip, "It could probably be shown by facts and figures that there is no distinctively native American criminal class except Congress."

What happens when a government makes unjust laws or tramples on people's inalienable rights? In a representative republic, we have a voice in government through our representatives, as well as a right to speak out, to petition the government, and to work to change laws. In our first session, we saw this in the example of Rev. Dr. Martin Luther King Jr.; we can add other examples such as William Wilberforce, the great British parliamentarian who fought tirelessly for decades for the abolition of the slave trade and ultimately of slavery itself in the British Empire. Wilberforce is a particularly interesting example because he won in Parliament by building a broad-based consensus for abolition in the society, which allowed pro-abolition parliamentarians to be elected and made abolition ultimately inevitable.

Vigorous advocacy

Both King and Wilberforce illustrate the importance of vigorous advocacy for moral and ethical issues in the public square. As we consider ethical problems, whether in government or in any other sphere, it is important to remember that fundamental change happens only when there is a widespread movement that values ethics more than the supposed benefits that come from ethical compromises. And building that consensus requires people who are willing to speak out in favor of a high view of human life and liberty in our families, in our neighborhoods, and in the public square. As Edmund Burke observed, "All that is necessary for the triumph of evil is that good men do nothing."

VIDEO NOTES OUTLINE

I. The Purpose of Government

    A. Inalienable rights

    B. Limited government

II. Justice

    A. Distributive justice

    B. Subsidiarity

    C. Retributive justice

III. Government and the moral law

    A. Promoting virtue

    B. Wilberforce

    C. Bonhoeffer

IV. Culture and evil

    A. Abandoning the ethic of life

    B. Desensitization

    C. The Manhattan Declaration

V. Changing the culture

   A. Free speech

   B. Politics downstream from culture

   C. Patience

   D. Danger of utopias

VI. Responding to relativism

SUBSIDIARITY is the principle that says that issues should be dealt with at as local and decentralized a level as possible. In other words, the central government should play a subsidiary role, handling only those tasks that cannot be performed on a more local level. As a social principle, families, civic organizations, and churches are more "local" to many issues than even the local government. As a result, they should deal with any issues they can without government involvement. Only problems they cannot solve should be taken up by any government entity, and then only by the lowest level that can address the situation effectively.

DIETRICH BONHOEFFER (1906 – 1945) was a brilliant German pastor and theologian who was a leader of the Confessing Church, the major source of Christian opposition to the Nazis in Germany itself. He worked as a double agent within the *Abwehr* (a German military intelligence group) and was ultimately executed for his involvement in a plot to assassinate Hitler.

QUESTIONS:

For Group Discussion

1. **Discuss:** Read Romans 13:1–5; 1 Timothy 2:1–4; and 1 Peter 2:13–14. According to these Scripture passages, what are the legitimate functions of government? Do you think government's functions should be limited, or can it take on responsibilities in any area it thinks appropriate?

2. **Consider:** There are a number of relatively new terms related to justice in use today, such as social justice, environmental justice, and economic justice. Many insist that these are legitimate areas of justice and thus the responsibility of the government.

   Discuss: How do you define justice? How does retributive justice fit within your definition? What about distributive justice? Do you think government should be responsible for the areas of justice outlined above or should the government limit itself to the more traditional, narrow concept of justice? Explain your answer.

   How does the principle of subsidiarity (see definition on previous page) apply to these areas?

3. **Consider:** People frequently say that you can't legislate morality; in other words, you can't make laws based on moral principles because law can't make people moral. Michael Miller, however, argues that all law is the legislation of morality. It's hard to see how law can be anything other than the legislating of morality. We all agree that laws against murder or theft are legitimate, even if they are based on natural law ethics (that is, they "legislate morality").

   Discuss: Can or should we put all aspects of natural law ethics into our law codes? If not, which moral issues should be left to the purely private sphere? Why? Do you think law should promote virtue, or should it simply restrain vice? If it should promote virtue, how would it do so?

4. **Discuss:** When government is promoting or tolerating grave injustices such as slavery or apartheid, what should be our response? When should we move beyond advocacy for change to civil disobedience? Is it ever legitimate to move to armed insurrection (such as the American Revolution)?

   Do you think our government is tolerating grave injustices today? If so, what evils do you see? In light of your answer in the first part of this question, what should be our response? Will you do what you are advocating?

5. **Consider:** Glenn Sunshine said that politics is downstream from culture, and argued that the only way to lasting change in society is through building a broad-based consensus that will drive political change. Robert George argued that when the government is supporting policies we believe to be unethical, we need to get involved, particularly by exercising our right to free speech and working to persuade those in our sphere of influence of our position.

Discuss: In your experience, can you freely advocate for moral and ethical positions in discussions of public policy, or are some views effectively censored? Are religious arguments welcome in dealing with political matters? Does it matter which religious viewpoint is being expressed? If you think expressing some viewpoints is taboo, how should we respond?

QUESTIONS:

For Individual Reflection and Action in the Coming Days

1. What issues in public policy or justice do you think are particularly important right now? What can you do to move the culture in a more ethically sound direction on these issues? Are there political candidates you can support or legislators you can contact? Are there political advocacy groups you can join? Whom can you talk to about the issues? What action will you take to move the culture?

2. Read the Manhattan Declaration at www.manhattandeclaration.org. Consider signing it if you have not done so already.

3. What are the main ideas and conclusions you take away from these discussions of ethics? Can you see any ways in which your own thinking about ethical behavior is beginning to change?

4. The main message from this final session is that morality matters, particularly as it comes to expression in the public square. Therefore, "we the people" need to be vigilant over the public square, to ensure that sound ethics will guide the decisions of our

leaders and the policies of our nations. What are the implications of such a lesson for you?

5. At ColsonCenter.org, read one or two of the additional resources listed below. The URLs are provided for your convenience in finding these articles.

Additional Resources

"Politics and Religion," by Kerby Anderson:
   http://www.colsoncenter.org/search-library/search?view=searchdetail&id=13892

"Biblical Foundations of Limited Government," by Doug Bandow:
   http://www.colsoncenter.org/search-library/search?view=searchdetail&id=13560

"Enlightened Ethics? The Failure of Secular Morality," by Charles Colson:
   http://www.colsoncenter.org/search-library/search?view=searchdetail&id=173

ADDITIONAL RESOURCES

Amazing Grace (2006), a film about the life of William Wilberforce and the fight to abolish the slave trade in the British Empire.

Amazing Grace: William Wilberforce and the Heroic Campaign to End Slavery, Eric Metaxas (Harper Collins, 2007).

BioEngagement: Making a Christian Difference through Bioethics Today, edited by Nigel M. de S. Cameron, Scott E. Daniels, and Barbara J. White (Eerdmans, 2000).

Bonhoeffer: Pastor, Martyr, Prophet, Spy, Eric Metaxas (Thomas Nelson, 2010).

The Call of the Entrepreneur. DVD with study guide (Acton Institute for the Study of Religion and Liberty, 2007).

The Commercial Society: Foundations and Challenges in a Global Age, Samuel Gregg (Lexington Books, 2007).

Crime and Human Nature: The Definitive Study of the Causes of Crime, James Q. Wilson and Richard J. Herrnstein (Simon and Schuster, 1985; Fress Press, 1998).

Gattaca (1997), a film which explores a world in which genetic testing determines your place in society.

God and Government, Charles W. Colson (Zondervan, 2007).

Human Dignity in the Biotech Century, edited by Charles W. Colson and Nigel M. de S. Cameron (InterVarsity Press, 2004).

Inside the Criminal Mind, revised and updated edition, Stanton E. Samenow (Crown, 2004).

Money, Greed, and God, Jay Richards (Harper Collins, 2009).

Natural Law: The Foundation of an Orderly Economic System, Alberto M. Piedra (Lexington Books, 2004).

Wall Street (2007), a film which explores what happens when greed becomes the sole motive in business.

Online Resources to Supplement This Study May Be Found at

www.DoingtheRightThing.com

> *"A man without ethics is a wild beast loosed upon the world"* — *Albert Camus*

www.DoingtheRightThing.com

Our goal is to spark a movement for ethical renewal with this video series. Indeed, we have indications that such a movement is already taking place across America. You aren't the only person with concerns about the problems in our bank-ing, legal, medical, teaching, and political professions, as well as within the church itself.

Only if we all start to spread the word, teach the young, and reinforce our own ethics with supportive local communities can we build a force that will reshape our culture for the better.

While *Doing the Right Thing* contains valuable lessons for any career path, we believe the discussions resulting from viewing this series is especially relevant to the following vocations, which have an enormous impact on our culture.

Business leaders
Medical professionals
College professors
Other educators

Two other groups have an enormous impact on the young as well as their own peers at church or in other community groups.

Homeschool parents
Small group leaders

Whether you want to lead a "Doing the Right Thing" discussion in your home among friends, work colleagues, church members, or perhaps open your home to a college group, any effort that raises America's consciousness, block by block, community by community can add to the movement.

There are many more resources available for free online. Please visit www.DoingtheRightThing.com to access these and for more information.

Other Small Group Studies and Resources from the Colson Center for Christian Worldview

The Faith
In this powerful curriculum, Chuck Colson and Gabe Lyons identify the unshakable tenets of the faith that Christians have believed through the centuries—truths that offer a ground for faith in uncertain times, hope and joy for those who despair, and reconciliation for a world at war with God and itself.

Chuck Colson on Politics and the Christian Faith
From his time as counsel to President Richard Nixon to his years as commentator on the radio broadcast *Breakpoint* and his leadership of Prison Fellowship, Chuck Colson is uniquely qualified to provide an insider's perspective on today's pressing issues of faith and politics. This four-session DVD curriculum gives individuals or small groups the opportunity to hear neither a "religious right" nor a "religious left" perspective, but balanced, clear, and biblically based thoughts on these important issues. Colson provides a great starting point for informed and thoughtful discussion and application to life in a political world.

Wide Angle
Chuck Colson and Pastor Rick Warren tackle some of the key issues of our day: truth vs. relativism, creationism vs. Darwinism, tolerance, terrorism, and so much more. You will learn about competing worldviews, the biblical basis for a Christian worldview, and its application to every facet of life.

Rewired
Chuck Colson and Teen Mania partnered to create the *Rewired* worldview curriculum to teach teens *how* to think Christianly. A relationship with Jesus is more than Scripture memorization and Sunday church attendance. Knowing Christ radically alters the way we understand life, the world, and all reality. It's a total worldview. And when teens have a Christian worldview, they will better understand how to integrate their faith into every aspect of their lives.

Centurions Program
The Centurions Program prepares Christians to live out their faith authentically and powerfully in the world and unites them in an ongoing and growing network of worldview movement leaders. As believers apply biblical truth to every aspect of their lives—becoming more like Christ in how they think and act—they will serve as catalysts for redemption in their homes, workplaces, churches, communities, and culture.

For these and other resources visit
http://www.breakpoint.org/resources

Share Your Thoughts

With the Author: Your comments will be forwarded to the author when you send them to *zauthor@zondervan.com*.

With Zondervan: Submit your review of this book by writing to *zreview@zondervan.com*.

Free Online Resources at
www.zondervan.com

Zondervan AuthorTracker: Be notified whenever your favorite authors publish new books, go on tour, or post an update about what's happening in their lives at www.zondervan.com/authortracker.

Daily Bible Verses and Devotions: Enrich your life with daily Bible verses or devotions that help you start every morning focused on God. Visit www.zondervan.com/newsletters.

Free Email Publications: Sign up for newsletters on Christian living, academic resources, church ministry, fiction, children's resources, and more. Visit www.zondervan.com/newsletters.

Zondervan Bible Search: Find and compare Bible passages in a variety of translations at www.zondervanbiblesearch.com.

Other Benefits: Register yourself to receive online benefits like coupons and special offers, or to participate in research.

ZONDERVAN.com/
AUTHORTRACKER
follow your favorite authors